King's Lynn In Colour
1960s to 1980s
(Volume 1)

Tricky Sam Publishing

Copyright © Bob Booth 2014

First Printed 2014

Email: trickysampublishing@tiscali.co.uk
Website: www.trickysampublishing.co.uk

All rights reserved.
No part of this publication may be reproduced in any form without prior permission from the publisher.

Acknowledgements

The quality of the photographs varies owing to many different sources, although I must give special thanks to Barry Williamson and all the staff at Norfolk Museum Services in Lynn as many of the photos are from their collections.

I must also stress that, although I have tried to give accurate descriptions and dates, invariably I cannot guarantee the validity of some of these. I hope you will enjoy the book for the nostalgia it brings. This is not meant to be a definitive historical work but a fond look back on our town and, maybe, the pictures will invoke your own (hopefully happy) memories.

The copyright of photographs from the Lynn News, West Norfolk Borough Council and the Eastern Daily Press is acknowledged and gratefully appreciated. A special thanks to all the staff at the Norfolk County Council Library & Information Service, King's Lynn for all their help to the author, Colin Bailey of Fraser Dawbarns for his legal expertise, John Allen for proof reading and valuable advice, all the staff at Clanpress and to Janet for her help with layout, cover design and support. And to all those who have offered me help over the last few years.

Left: Lower Canada (between St James Girls school and the railway yard and station) disappears in 1966.
Centre: The Barley Mow pub on Railway Road disappears to make way for Oldsunway rear access road to the new shopping precinct in 1972.
Right: The neat row of houses in Bedford Street, along with Stanley Street, Marshall Street and Kirby Street (off Railway Road) will all go in 1976.

2

Introduction

The town has always seen demolition of the old and building of the new. As the population of the town expanded, particularly with the advent of the 'London overspill', there was a large scale building of new homes and retail development of (mainly) two streets - Broad Street and New Conduit Street - which at best could have been described as secondary in terms of retail before the late 1960s.

Following the major slum clearance of the 1930s more town communities were deemed (in some cases arguably) to be unfit for habitation and disappeared off the town map during the late 1950s through to the 1970s.Compare the number of streets in the town with that of 80 years ago when the vast majority of the population lived within the town walls (*King's Lynn Street Directory, 1933 - still available*)

The biggest change to the town landscape was about to start in 1966 when the new style town centre plans were approved for the building of new retail units in the two aforementioned streets. By January 1967 there was objection by shopkeepers in the central area covering New Conduit Street, Broad Street and part of Norfolk Street who were served with compulsory purchase orders calling it 'dictatorship of the worst kind'. It was planned to provide about sixty shop units and offices.

Twenty nine shopkeepers met the Lynn Chamber of Trade (who, incidentally, were supposed to support their members) - to no avail as the plan was to develop a pedestrianised New Conduit Street and Broad Street through an arcade, a multi-storey car park for 850 cars in the cattle market area together with a new bus terminus. The developers (Second Covent Garden Co.) wanted to start building by March 1st 1967.

Like the owners of homes in many compulsorily purchased areas in town, businesses were bought for well below the true market value.

Above left: Highgate being demolished in 1957.

Centre: North End looking from the bottom of Pilot Street in 1960 and demolition has begun in North Street while St Nicholas Chapel stands defiantly.

Right: Chapel Lane (North End) looking from Austin Street in its last year before it disappears (except No.8 at the bottom) in 1959.

By the late 1950s it was decided by the Town Council that certain areas of the town should be made subject to wholesale clearance even if properties could/should have been saved and modernised. Whereas the 1930s slum clearance could be justified, much of the areas demolished from the late 1950s had the basic facilities of running water and individual toilets and the buildings were reasonably sound and, with some investment, could be made perfectly habitable. Thus preserving the historic fabric of the town. Instead many householders were served with compulsory purchase notices and offered only a few hundred pounds as compensation. The main residential areas lost included: Highgate, most of North End, Lower Canada, the areas around South Clough Lane, Kirby Street, Windsor Road and the whole area now taken up by Hillington Square.

ABOVE: Left to right (the area to become Hillington Square): Morgan's Brewery (1963), Providence Street to Millfleet (1966), All Saint's Street (north side) (1966). The south side of All Saint's Street escaped demolition.

ABOVE: Left: Described as an anachronism amid the 'brave new world' in 1969, the 1880s built South Clough Lane area with few houses still occupied. *Centre:* By 1971 the site is cleared. *Right:* Kirby Street area, as far west as Railway Road, is being demolished in 1976.

4

PROTESTS BY NORTH END

A MINISTRY of Housing inspector conducted a public inquiry on Tuesday into Lynn Town Council's clearance order made in respect of North Street and Pilot Street.

The inspector was told that the people of North End might not be a handsome lot, but they were a tough lot, and a number of them turned up to protest.

ABOVE: The wreckers turn their attention to St Nicholas Street supposedly to make way for a road improvement scheme to align with Austin Street to join directly to the Tuesday Market Place while the rest of the site down to Market Lane was to be redeveloped as offices 'immediately'. William White's house (on the corner of Chapel and St Nicholas Street) plus the Lattice House and adjoining cottages would be preserved. In the end the alignment didn't happen and the site is now just a car park.

ABOVE: The corner of Norfolk Street and Broad Street and the Grosvenor and Fiddaman's have been reduced to a heap of rubble in 1969.

FIDDAMAN'S NOT TO BE REBUILT

FIDDAMAN'S HOTEL, WHICH BEFORE ITS DEMOLITION LAST YEAR WAS ONE OF LYNN'S MOST DISTINCTIVE PUBLIC HOUSES, IS NOT TO BE REBUILT.

Lynn News 1968 - Fiddaman's RIP

Left: To add insult to injury (my grandmother was offered £50 for her house in Chapel Lane). Northenders were referred to as "not a handsome lot" - an insult to my family and everyone else of North End heritage. The demolition would include North Street, Pilot Street (west side), True's Yard, North Place, Begley's Yard, Whitening Yard and Allen's Yard also Austin Street and much of Albert Street and associated yards. A house owner living in North Street, said at an inquiry that he had bought his house eight years previously as a home. He and his wife thought that they would spend the rest of their lives there and that they did not want to move. He also said *"They call this a free country. There is no freedom if a man has got to pull down his own home".*

The fact that a man bought his home suggests that many of the properties were in good condition and not slum properties that needed demolishing.

RIGHT:
By 1972 North End was virtually flattened as highlighted by the Lynn News headline. But thanks to all at True's Yard the memory will never die!

BOTTOM RIGHT:
The area to the north of New Conduit Street in 1967 where once stood a Congregational Church is being cleared for the new shop development by Second Covent Garden and Lynn Town Council.

Spirit has gone from nostalgic North End scene

GATEWAY TO PROGRESS

ABOVE: The Youth Centre in Tower Street was demolished in 1970 in order to make way for an access road.

The building which was originally a Wesleyan Methodist school had been associated with the life of many generations of Lynn folk. The ornate cupola and weather vane crashes down in a ten ton heap of lead and brick.

RIGHT: The Duke of Edinburgh pub in 1973 on the corner of Littleport Street and Blackfriars Road along with two Edwardian properties are demolished to improve traffic movement but were replaced with flats instead.

LYNN NEWS & ADV

Incorporating LYNN ADVERTISER (1841) LYNN NEWS (1860)

Postage 6d. No. 12,264 FRIDAY, JANUARY 13, 1967.

LYNN TRADERS WILL FIGHT COMPULSION

'Dictatorship of the worst kind'

LYNN shopkeepers in the central area covering New Conduit Street, Broad Street and part of Norfolk Street, are to fight Lynn Town Council over the proposed compulsory purchase of their businesses and land to make way for the re-building and development of the area by the partnership of the council and the Second Covent Garden Property Co., Ltd.

They are supported in their action by other shopkeepers in Norfolk Street not affected by the development at this stage, 31 of whom have already formed themselves into a private traders protest group.

Compulsory purchase powers would apply and be served on all the businesses in this area despite the fact that many of these businesses owned their land and had traded (in some instances) very many years.

It would probably mean the traders (having been bought out) would have to lease property at an un-economic rent thus making it impossible to continue.

Another view was that this would mean more larger national traders leading to the end of the small trader. With rents expected to be around £3000 per annum most small traders could not survive.

Demolition of the cattle market in 1971. This would form the east side of shops in Broad Street.

6

High Street c1971 and, judging by the number of shoppers, it looks like a late summer Saturday morning. The distinctive frontage of Ladyman's has been replaced with the bland architecture which is now Littlewood's. Beyond Littlewood's is the International Tea Co. Ltd which would struggle on for another year against the rising tide of supermarkets. Next door is the other distinctive façade of Boots the Chemists which would become Timothy Whites (hardware retailers) in the next couple of years. Boots (who owned Timothy Whites) moved to a new unit built on the site of the old Scott & Son (furnishers) at 92/97 High Street. The Timothy White name eventually disappeared across the country in 1985.

The corner of High Street and Norfolk Street c1970. A nearly new Mini prepares to turn right towards the Tuesday Market Place (G reg plates were issued from August 1968 to July 1969), while a learner waits to turn left down High Street under the tutelage of an 'Auto' school of motoring instructor. A Grammar school boy appears to be heading straight across to Woolworths.

Left of picture: Richard Shops at 115-117 High Street. In 1958 the original Richard Shops on this site was demolished and this new unit was built - seen above in the 1972.
Middle background is Tesco, which is now trading in what was Le Grice Bros Ltd (fashions, fabrics, furnishings & general drapery).
Just beyond Tesco is WH Smith. The updating of the frontage of Jermyn's has also been recently completed. Within the next year Jermyn's would become Debenham's.

At the junction of High Street, New Conduit Street and Purfleet Street circa 1969 a young couple out shopping appear oblivious of a Ford Cortina behind. A Police 'Panda' car (Hillman Imp) heads towards the Saturday Market Place. These small/medium size cars were known as Panda cars owing to the white band with black writing. The scaffolding on the extreme left indicates the construction of the new development (Cantor's) in New Conduit Street.

10

Blackfriars Street looking east towards 'Steven's Corner' (the junction with Railway Road and St James Road) in 1975. The gap in the street had been a confectioners and private house. The newer building next door, (nearer to the photographer) had been a large three storey semi-detached residence and now reappears as a shop unit.

The corner of Broad Street looking north towards Norfolk Street in c1967. Maddison Andree a well known hairdressers in the 1960s was housed in the Broad Street Chambers. Just beyond Maison Andree is John Slator' (ironmongers) and a VW Beetle stands outside Sexton Bros. (fruit merchants). In the past the chambers had been home to The National Telephone Co., Miles and Son (estate agents), and the East Anglian Trustees Savings Bank.

Broad Street looking south towards the GPO in 1967. By now the cattle market had moved and was used as a car park. The shops from the market down to the GPO were: Reeds (newsagents), the Anglia Restaurant, King's Lynn Press, Spare Moments (wool shop), Lynn Fruit & Flowers (fruiterers), Rosaline Bucke (gowns), Avery (scale makers), Miss Chilvers (baby linen), Lynn Labour Party office, and Whisky-a-Go Go (café).

13

Broad Street c1968. Looking towards Norfolk Street from the Cattle Market. The Cattle Market Tavern (closed May 1964) was replaced by Green & Wright (opened November 1965) - next to Baptist's Yard. The other side of the yard is N Mayes (second-hand dealer). Further down and next to the entrance to Bath's Yard are the new units of Frost & Walsh and Pratt & Coldham.
By about 1970 the whole street had disappeared to make way for the (then) new shopping centre.

A view of New Conduit Street from Baxter's Plain looking towards High Street c1967. Just visible behind the trees is the old British Restaurant, at this time the High School canteen. The white imitation (stuccoed and scribed) stone-faced building on the corner of Baxter's Plain and New Conduit Street is Essex & Suffolk Insurance Co. Ltd. Next door is Giffard Page (antiques) and DER (television rental).

New Conduit Street looking towards Baxter's Plain in winter 1966. A sign in the grounds of the Congregational Church announce the impending demolition and redevelopment of the street - by Autumn 1969 new shop building along here was well advanced. Only a small section of the street (at the North end leading from High Street) has survived (see opposite).

Another picture taken at the same time showing (on the left) the properties that survived the demolition onslaught. At this time New Conduit Street had far fewer retail outlets than any of the other main shopping streets but this all changed with the advent of the new development. The buildings on the left down to the Sun & Alliance Insurance Group have survived to this day.

Railway Road at the junction with Norfolk Street and John Kennedy Way in September 1968. This junction was generally referred to as Townsend's Corner after Charles Townsend Ltd (corn merchant), out of view to the right of picture, until 1964 when this 'T' junction became a cross-road on the opening of John Kennedy Way. The shadows indicate that it is probably late afternoon and possibly a Wednesday. Flower Corner was listed as 49 Norfolk Street. Next to that is H&R Hatton (newsagents) 63/64 Railway Road - next to Townsend's Corner bus-stop. Just beyond is the Crystal Palace pub.

Railway Road looking north from Wellesley Street (right) and Albion Street (left). The year is 1968 and it's four years since Townsends Corner disappeared and John Kennedy Road had opened as the first part of the extension leading to the northern bypass. A bus is pulling away from what was Townsend's Corner on its way to Steven's Corner and then to the Millfleet where it will terminate. Townsend's Corner bus stops were probably the busiest for passengers to alight and disembark.

St James' Road in March 1968. This formed the eastern boundary of the South Clough Lane area - Tower Street forming the western boundary. To the right of picture (out of view) is St James' Park and ahead is the junction with Blackfriars Street. The site where these properties stand is now the town swimming pool and multi-storey car park.

The Flower Pot pub on the corner of Norfolk Street and Chapel Street in 1971. A Steward & Patteson pub (bought from Bagges brewery in 1929), it was taken over by Watney Mann in February 1969 and then closed. With its distinctive brown brick and rounded corners this Victorian edifice was very pleasing on the eye although, in 1899, the original lower part of the frontage was destroyed when a very large cart carrying part of Barnum & Bailey's circus pulled by many horses collided with it.

21

This photo taken from near the junction with High Street shows Norfolk Street in 1969. The part of Marks & Spencer shown here had been added when the company had purchased the Mann Egerton garage in 1959. Plowright, Pratt and Harbage (ironmongers) is visible in the middle of the photo.

Further down Norfolk Street the Plowright's shop on the right is not the same branch seen on the opposite page but an electrical outlet of the same company. The Bird in Hand pub and the vacant lot next door, which had been Davy Bros. (drapers), was purchased some years later when George Goddard (tailors) moved from High Street.

Chapel Street in c1967. The road junction on the right is Austin Street, ahead is the junction with St Ann's and St Nicholas Streets. S Wheatley was a general grocers where my Grandma sent me on errands from her house in Chapel Lane (about 100 yards up Austin Street). Next to Wheatley's was Florence (baby linen). On the left of the picture is Eastern Counties Utilities (King's Lynn) Ltd (motor accessories).

Tower Street c1966. Dees bought Bambridges (fruiterers) at 17, Tower Street in the late 1950s then expanded to include 19, Tower Street and then 15, Tower Street. Both these businesses had been fishmongers.

By 1968 Dees ceased trading and the whole site became home to the East Anglian Trustee Savings Bank which had moved from High Street.

The bank eventually became the TSB.

Next door to Dees is C McLean (wallpaper & paint) and just beyond slightly set back is W Bush (fish & chips) whilst the brown brick property is a private dwelling (Whincop House).

Further down the yellow frontage shop is Watts & Rowe (printers and stationers). Just before that and well set back is the Youth Centre (an old Methodist Church School) - today a road (Regent Way) goes through here.

The blue green building is the Rummer Hotel (a favourite with bingo fans from the Theatre Royal).

Bayes, Tower Street in July 1964. The shop had previously been a radio and TV shop owned by my father. I had moved to this shop in 1963 having started above his shop in St James Street in 1957 whilst still at school. Jim Reeves (advertised on the window) had just entered the pop chart at No.5 in July. Upstairs was our recording studio - a room with some very basic recording equipment. Here virtually every local (and not so local) band recorded. Next door (right) was the Golden Ball pub. In 1965 Janet joined me and in 1967 we bought the business from my father. In 1973 we moved to Broad Street.

26

London Road in the early-mid 1970s. A Bentley is passing Eric Batterham's hairdressers at No.4, London Road and the confectioners at No. 2 which was owned by Mrs I Bullen. The elegant house at No. 1 just pre-dates the Victorian age by a couple of years. Just out of sight to the left of the photographer is the town library.

27

London Road in the 1960s. Barwell Rubber Co. Ltd. (tyre rebuilders & distributors) occupied 16, London Road next to the entrance to Hospital Walk. In 1968 the business was acquired by Kevin Shortis who had started his business in Norwich. He hoisted a Mini onto the roof to gain maximum notice of his business! Today the Shortis Group (Wilco and Fast-Fit) is one of the largest motor spares parts companies in the country.

28

South Lynn Plain in April 1967. The pub on the corner of Church Lane is the Anchor Inn. On the other corner of Church Lane and All Saints Street is AW Arrowsmith (butcher). At the bottom of Church Lane is All Saints Church and St Mary's School. The bay window on the left of picture is FJ Cozens (secondhand dealer). Behind the photographer is Friars Street.
To the right of picture further up South Lynn Plain is Valinger's Road which leads down to London Road.

Wisbech Road 1964. This row of shops is opposite the now extinct gasworks which closed in 1964 with the advent of natural gas from the North Sea. The gas produced at the gasworks was used to supply the town. This process of coal distillation (not burning) also produced coke, coal tar and ammonia. The coke can be used for heating while coal tar can be separately distilled to produce various oils from which many pharmaceuticals and fuels can be produced. Ammonia was converted to produce fertiliser.
Since our country is short of fuel (relying on other countries) and we have plenty of coal, perhaps this process is worth revisiting.

30

Chilvers Brothers was in Littleport Street on the corner of Austin Street (often referred to as 'Chilver's Corner') and was advertised as cycle agents. As seen in photo cycle sales was the main business and to the left of the shop was a sizeable repair workshop. The petrol pump in the picture also indicated that cars could be filled up as well. Right of picture is RG Carter (builders & contractors) – the opening also leads to Modern Butter Packers Ltd.

Alfred Dodman & Co Ltd (boiler makers, general engineers, ship repairers and canning machinery manufacturers) occupied a large site on Gaywood Road next to the railway line to the docks. Not surprisingly the bridge over the dock line has always been (and still is by locals) referred to as 'Dodman's bridge'. The company finally closed in the late 1970s.

Wootton Road c1966.

Allen & Neale (chemists) had their main business in High Street. In the 1930s Arthur Marsters occupied the whole of the building (No. 3, Wootton Road) and traded as a grocer.
From the titles on the façia the business was Gaywood's own supermarket.

KLCS at 5, Wootton Road is the King's Lynn & District Co-operative Society Ltd. (butchery department).

Just beyond is River Lane (inset below). Just beyond these hoardings was (and still is) the renowned River Lane Fish & Chip shop.
The off white building is the White Horse public house.

Opposite page: Blake Bros (cycle dealers) were at 347, Wootton Road next to Malt Row. From the signage on the van they also delivered paraffin - at this time (mid 1960s) many people still used paraffin (incidently obtain by distilling coal) for heating and cooking. They were experts on cycles and were also blacksmiths.

This page: Next door to Blakes was the New Inn pub - the last pub out of town on the Hunstanton - Fakenham roads as the sign indicates. The building on the left could be hired for parties, wedding receptions etc. At this time Hunstanton traffic went through Castle Rising as the bypass from Hardwick to Babingley was under construction (started 1964) but had not yet been completed. The road marked North Wootton is now part of the northern bypass into town (avoiding Gaywood).

BLAKE'S
CYCLES & HARDWARE
347 WOOTTON ROAD KING'S LYNN
PINK PARAFFIN DELIVERY SERVICE
DULUX

LEFT: King's Lynn Junction signal box. The driver passes the daily paper to the signalman as he departs with an early train bound for Liverpool Street in 1982.

RIGHT: In 1983 the signalman at Harbour Junction box hands over a fresh brew for the driver who has just left South Lynn yard and is joining the main line with empty wagons from the British Sugar beet factory bound for the Lynn goods yard.

The front of King's Lynn station, Blackfriars Road, in 1970. The parcels office is at the left-hand end. A grey Ford Zephyr passes the station while an orange Hillman Imp and a two tone Vauxhall Cresta stand outside. The first station, virtually just a wooden shed, was built in October 1846 on a site a few yards north of the present station which opened in March 1871. The new King's Lynn station (known as just 'Lynn' until 1871) was built as a joint venture by the Great Eastern Railway, the Midland Railway and the Great Northern Railway.
The station has just been totally refurbished (2014) and looks better than it has for years - probably since it was first built.

Portland Street looking towards Railway Road from Blackfriars Road in February 1968. The East Anglian Hotel on the left and houses beyond (at ground floor level) have imitation stonework and the first floor windows have decorative moulded hoods. In the mid 19th century the railway company had owned the land where Portland Street now stands as it intended to extend nearer to the town and the cattle market and build a new station but it ran into serious debt and had to scrap the plan. Thus the anomaly of the railway station being some 100yards from Railway Road.

Guanock Terrace looking towards Guanock Place and London Road in February 1976. The pub was built in the mid 19th century and named Queen Caroline (named after the wife of George IV - the name was changed to Lord Napier (a British diplomat) in 1869.

South Quay in July 1975. The Bell Crusader, built on the Clyde in 1956, although registered in Limassol, Cyprus was actually owned by Bell Lines of Dublin. On this trip she would be loaded with 1423 tons of Norfolk barley. The reason she was registered in Cyprus and not Eire was that it was a cheaper option - known as a flag of convenience.

The Fisher Fleet at low tide. There is no date for this picture but from the size of the boats (a far cry from today's leviathans) it must be 1960s/1970s. In the1940s my Grandad Bob Booth and his brother invented a winch for hauling in the nets by using the power of the boat's engine rather than having to haul the net in by hand. Most boats in the fleet (like those above) eventually had one built and fitted by Grandad and his brother - in their spare time. At that time most people worked a $5\frac{1}{2}$ day week - with one week's paid holiday per year! The boat in the foreground has a port code LT indicating it is registered in Lowestoft, while LN is the code for Lynn. Since LynN was LN then LondoN was coded LO. It was usual to use the first and last letter of the port. Apparently this meant that London was of less significance than Lynn when the system was devised - so I was once told by a seaman!

In 1967 the south side of All Saints Street stands defiantly while the north side is being demolished to make way for the new Hillington Square development. The Union Street sign can be seen partially obscured by a tree. This street ran down to Coronation Square. Further down the street the white building on the corner (the Anchor Inn) is at the junction with Church Lane and South Lynn Plain.

42

Archdale Street in 1975. Little has changed other than the cars! It leads from Eastgate Street (off Gaywood Road) at the bottom of 'Dodman's Bridge'. Note the immaculately maintained properties.

St. James' Street in February 1967. The Cadenza café (with red illuminated sign) had only just been opened by Lynn-O-Matics (games machines and juke boxes). Janet and I (as programmer / suppliers of records for all their juke boxes) were invited to an official opening one evening in March 1967. There was concern that one particular record we had just supplied all their boxes with would flop as would the group with such a quirky name who sang about a man who stole from ladies washing lines - it went on to be a firm favourite and was the most played on all their boxes over the next few months. The record was 'Arnold Layne' by Pink Floyd!

South Clough Lane looking towards St James Road and the Park c1968. The sun streams down Bentinck Street leading off on the right. The boarded up shop was a general shop and before that had been a fish & chip shop. Within the next year or so the whole site would disappear.

In October 1967 the morning sun streams down Regent Street which ran from South Clough Lane to this point where it met Regent Place (through the passage ahead) and Whincop Street (next to the house on the right). Regent Place met St. James Street beside the Police Station. The large building in the picture is the Independent Club.

Paradise Parade looking from the corner of the cattle market towards Baxter's Plain in c1968. The General Post Office is on the left of the photo. Note the classic rounded brown brick façade of Bond & Easter (auctioneers, valuers and estate agents) who, by this time, had ceased trading.

Albion Street in 1967 looking north from Market Street - the Lord Kelvin pub is behind the photographer. On the left of the street is the old St John's Primary and Infant school. It had opened in 1853 after the institution of the new Poor Law when the government provided sums of money to build schools in order to educate poor children (*'King's Lynn Schools'* published in 2011 gives details of all Lynn schools). The far end of the street is the corner of the cattle market.

The Walks, along with the town swimming pool (or baths) and the paddling pool to cool off on a hot summer day, was a favourite area particularly for children and teenagers. In the background is Tennyson Road - a continuation of Tennyson Avenue. The wooden structure was the ladies' changing cubicles - the men's cubicles were at the other end of the pool with the entrance in the middle. A season ticket for me in 1950s would cost my parents 10/- and used just about every day was good value!
There was a board at the entrance showing the water temperature - the lowest I remember was 48°F/9°C (freezing) and the highest 72°F/22°C (heaven)!

The Millfleet, at the end of Stonegate Street, circa late 1970s. The bridge seen has been bricked up after the Millfleet was ducted and filled in at the turn of the 20th century.

The bridge had been the southern entrance to the town and was known as Lady Bridge.

The new flats in the picture are part of Hillington Square which had replaced Morgan's Ladybridge brewery.

The name was derived from 'Our Lady' chapel which had stood here before 1806.

The ubiquitous supermarket trolleys and other detritus do not make a good impression on visitors to the town and its long illustrious history.

CHURCH STREET

In 1968 at 15, Church Street (next to St Margaret's churchyard) was the premises of Edward Jermyn (house furnisher).

Above his shop at 15a was HG ('Horrie') Britton (radio, TV and cycle dealer). His doorway can clearly be seen but the premises must have been very cramped if he was stocking radios, TVs and bicycles, not to mention lugging these large items up and down the narrow stairs!

Next door is an Insurance Brokers.

This picture of the Duke's Head Hotel and National Provincial Bank (4, Tuesday Market Place) was probably taken one peaceful Sunday morning in 1950s. The blue painted façade of the hotel has virtually been washed away over the years. Soon it would be re-painted in a less tasteful pink until it was re-painted in blue recently. The National Provincial Bank amalgamated with the Westminster Bank (8, Tuesday Market Place) to become the National Westminster Bank (Natwest) in 1970. By 1973 the branch at No.8 had closed.
For some strange reason the right-hand third of the hotel was occupied by Barclays Bank through the 1930s.

52

The junction of Austin Street, Norfolk Street, Blackfriars Road and Littleport Street in 1967. A scooter emerges from Blackfriars Road while a learner driver turns into Littleport Street. This junction has changed little over time except the traffic priorities are now different and it is obviously far busier today than it was fifty years ago.

Just along from Scaifes in Norfolk Street is Limbert's (fish and chips) - a lady can be seen walking past - and every Saturday I would queue here to get our Saturday dinner since we only lived 100 yards or so away towards the Railway Station.

By the late 1960s much of the Cattle Market became derelict before finally the last live stock sale took place in June 1971. Catleughs' premises backed on to this corner of the market and the wall served as a good advertising surface - probably for the better off farmers!

54

Mrs F Sullivan's shop in Coronation Square is probably in her last year of trading in the mid 1960s before the whole of the area is cleared to make way for the new Hillington Square.

The shop had only been the archetypal corner grocery/general shop since the mid 1950s.

Before that 23, Coronation Square was the premises of a wardrobe dealer and before the war a fishmonger *(see King's Lynn, Illustrated Street Directory of 1933).*

The lane to the right is Crooked Lane that ran through to Bridge Street which, in the late 1940s still retained derelict buildings from bomb damage in 1942.

After school (St James Boys in Hospital Walk) this area, along with the area around the Nar [with the railway sidings] was our play-ground. Those who dared would venture into the bombed out shells and run to the top of the buildings to wave to those of us not-so-brave watching from below.

When I was 13 years old I would pass this shop most evenings after working in the chemistry lab for my mentor Doc Lankshear in Union Street.

The whole area down to the river had its individual smells from crumbling brick-work to the brewery, the smell of steam engines and hot oil, maltings, grain on the South Quay, the waft of processing sugar beet and dozens more, not to mention all the associated sounds.

Why is everything so sterile today?

55

Where's Granville?

The scene evokes memories of 'Open All Hours'. 1968 - Smith Bros. (grocer & baker) at 237, Saddlebow Road. The shop was on the corner of Sydney Terrace and not far from South Lynn Station - which had closed to passengers in February 1959.

Just before the station at 277, Saddlebow Road was Smith Bros bakery.

This shop epitomised the typical corner shop of which there were about 75 in Lynn that went under the title of 'grocers' or 'shopkeepers'. The personal friendly service gave way to the impersonal supermarkets from the 1960s on.

South Everard Street in 1966. Eastwoods was a general builders merchant which was next door to the Bowling Green pub whose frontage was in Checker Street. Out of sight to the right was All Saints Infants and Primary Girls school which would close in 1974 and the pupils transfer to Whitefriars school.

South Gates roundabout (on the left) varied in size many times through the 1950s and 1960s - the roundabout in the photo had been extended from small in March 1960.

Before the bypass round the town traffic from the south and west had to pass through this point in order to reach the north-west Norfolk coast. In the summer the traffic going to Hunstanton could easily back up to the end of the Pullover Road and (from the north) even to Sutton Bridge at Bank Holiday times. Most trippers seemed to go from the roundabout down Vancouver Avenue only to experience long delays at Tennyson Avenue railway crossing where trains could be coming into the station every 7 minutes and then reversing out on the Hunstanton line.

58

Part of Queen Street in 1967 before demolition. The blue fronted building was a café until the mid 1960s but originally it was a pub (Union Jack) until 1933. The pub (the word 'Bagge' can just be made out in the tiling under the windows) had been the Ballast Boat from 1741 to 1893 when the name was changed. Bagge's brewery was taken over by Steward & Patteson.

St James Place in 1980. Down on the right is South Street and further down, Wood Street. Beyond is the corner of St James Park. The evening sun highlights what was once a general store (John Ess) but had closed in the mid 1960s to be briefly run by a Mrs E Brown in 1968 and finally closed in 1969. The pub, The Spotted Cow, now boarded up had closed in January 1967. The whole area is now flats and town houses surrounded on three sides by The Park and The Walks.

Nos. 3-5 North Street was the provision merchants of E Southgate & Sons. The photo was taken in March 1967. The sign above the shop states that this is also a 'ships chandler' although there is no evidence of this! This is now True's Yard Fisherfolk Museum.

61

Market Street in August 1967. The street opposite the Lord Kelvin pub is Albion Street. Further down Railway Road bisects this street and Waterloo Street and in the distance can be seen the railway station. This quiet street now sees all the buses that enter the bus fleet - the wall on the left having long been demolished. Mrs M Hutton's grocery shop next to the pub would continue for another year or two before closing.

62

Blackfriars Street in 1979. A rather bizarre exhibition when a giant whale could be viewed in a bus! According to the hoarding this was an educational exhibition on a world tour. If anyone expected to see a live whale in the bus then they would have been disappointed as (in small print) it was 'chemically preserved'. The shop on the left of the photo is Juby & Co Ltd (electrical contractors).

Location	Page	Location	Page
Albion Street	48	North Street	61
All Saints Street	42	Paradise Parade	47
Archdale Street	43	Portland Street	38
Austin Street	53	Queen Street	59
Blackfriars Road	37	Railway	36
Blackfriars Street	11, 63	Railway Road	18 - 19
Broad Street	12 - 14	Regent Street	46
Cattle Market	54	Saddlebow Road	56
Chapel Street	24	South Clough Lane	45
Church Street	51	South Everard Street	57
Coronation Square	55	South Gates	58
Fisher Fleet	41	South Lynn Plain	29
Gaywood Road	32	South Quay	40
Guanock Terrace	39	St James Place	60
High Street	7 - 10	St James Road	20
Littleport Street	31	St James Street	44
London Road	27 - 28	Tower Street	25 - 26
Market Street	62	Tuesday Market Place	52
Millfleet	50	Walks, The	49
New Conduit Street	15 - 17	Wisbech Road	30
Norfolk Street	21 - 23	Wootton Road	33 - 35